Health Zone

KEEP Your Cool!

What YOU Should KNOW about STRESS

Sandy Donovan

illustrations by Jack Desrocher

Consultant: Sonja Green, MD

Lerner Publications Company
Minneapolis

All characters in this book are fictional and are not based on actual persons. The characters' stories are not based on actual events. Any similarities thereof are purely coincidental.

Lerner Publications Company
A division of Lerner Publishing Group, Inc.
241 First Avenue North
Minneapolis, MN 55401 U.S.A.

Website address: www.lernerbooks.com

Library of Congress Cataloging-in-Publication Data

Donovan, Sandra, 1967–
 Keep your cool! : what you should know about stress / by Sandy Donovan ; illustrated by Jack Desrocher ; Consultant: Sonja Green.
     p. cm. – (Health zone)
 Includes bibliographical references and index.
 ISBN 978-0-8225-7555-9 (lib. bdg. : alk. paper)) 1. Stress management—Juvenile literature. 2. Stress management for children—Juvenile literature. I. Desrocher, Jack, ill. II. Green, Sonja. III. Title.
 RA785.L42 2009
 616.9′8-dc22
                                                          2007038858

Manufactured in the United States of America
2 3 4 5 6 7 — BP —   14 13 12 11 10 09

Table of Contents

Tara zipped up her jacket and grabbed her backpack.

Today was her first day at her new middle school.

Her family had moved from the other side of the city just a few weeks ago.

Tara and her brother loved their new house. And Tara's brother loved the neighborhood. He had already found a group of friends to play with. Today he was walking to his new school with his new friends. But Tara still hadn't met any new friends. Her mom told her she would make lots of friends once school started. Tara knew her mom was right. But that didn't make it any easier to go to school today without knowing one single person.

Tara had been dreading this day ever since she'd learned she was moving. She kept imagining how scary it would be to go into a new classroom and not recognize a single face.

What if no one liked her?

What if everyone already had all the friends they wanted?

What if the other kids made fun of her?

And what if she had nobody to sit with at lunch?

Tara usually made friends easily. But she couldn't help imagining the worst.

Last night, Tara could barely sleep. She kept tossing and turning, thinking about how afraid she was. This morning, nothing felt right. Her palms felt sweaty. Her mouth felt dry. Her whole body felt tense. Tara hardly ate any breakfast. She just wasn't hungry. She felt like she might burst into tears. Or maybe throw up. She could hardly tell what she felt anymore. It seemed like it was hard to even think straight. Now, walking out her front door, she could feel her heart racing and her hands trembling.

She wasn't sure how she was EVER going to make it through this day.

Chapter 1

WOUND UP
AND
Stressed
Out

Have you ever felt overwhelmed by something like the first day at a new school?

Like Tara, maybe your palms started sweating.

Or maybe you had butterflies in your stomach.

Even if you've never had to deal with being the new kid, you've still probably felt nervous about *something*. Lots of things can make kids nervous. Some kids get super worried every time they have to take a test. Others feel overwhelmed by homework, chores, and other activities. And some get worried about the people around them. They may worry that their parents are going to get divorced or lose their jobs or get too sick to take care of them.

In all of these situations, kids are experiencing stress.

You've probably heard people talk about how stressed they are about a million times, right? Adults get stressed, kids get stressed—even pets get stressed. Adults stress about their jobs. Kids stress about school. Both kids and adults stress about relationships and big events like family gatherings. Even the weather can stress people out.

But what exactly is stress? Is it bad for you? Good for you? **Can you do anything about it?** The answer to all of these questions is yes. To understand why stress is both good and bad for you and how you can control it, it helps to know exactly what stress is.

What Is Stress?

Lots of doctors and scientists study stress. They have different ideas about what stress is and what it does to your body. But everyone agrees that stress is the body's way of reacting to changes—either real changes or imagined changes. Any time something changes, you feel stress. In fact, if you even *think* something might change, you'll feel stress. Moving to a new neighborhood can obviously be stressful. Having your parents get divorced causes stress. But little events can be stressful too. **Trying out for a sports team can be stressful.** Feeling like you have a lot of homework can be stressful. Forgetting to do even a small homework assignment can lead to big stress for some kids.

Not All Stress Is the Same

Just like no two people are the same, no two stresses are the same. Some kids get stressed when too many things seem to be happening at once. Other kids get stressed when they feel like they can't control what's happening around them. And a lot of us experience stress that others are feeling. If your parents are stressed about money or something like that, you'll probably feel stress about it too.

Sounds pretty gloomy, doesn't it?

Does everybody just spend their whole life feeling stressed? _Luckily, no._ It's important to remember that there is good stress and bad stress. And there are ways to deal with both kinds of stress so they don't take over your life.

Stress **that comes from small events is often good for you.** The changes your body goes through help you deal with the stressful event. Imagine you're in the final minutes of playing your favorite fast–paced game. You probably feel all pumped up, right? Your palms might get sweaty. Your heart might start beating fast. You probably feel like you have extra energy. All of these symptoms of stress may actually help you play a little better. Whether you win or lose, these stress symptoms usually disappear soon after the game ends.

IT'S A FACT
Athletes usually feel
stressed right before a
game. The stress gives their
muscles extra energy to help
them play their best.

Stress Can Be Good: Carmen's Story

All year, Carmen had struggled in math class. So when her teacher announced that there was going to be a big final test, Carmen wanted to make sure she did well.

She began studying a week before the test. But as test day got nearer, she was nervous that she still hadn't studied enough. She canceled a trip to the movies with her friends so she could study. Her friends teased her a little and told her she was freaking out too much about one test. But Carmen knew that doing well was important to her. The night before the test, she didn't feel hungry at dinner. She made herself eat a few bites and then went straight to her room to study more. A couple hours later, her mom made her turn off her light. Carmen didn't feel tired. She worried that she should study more. But she figured she had done the best she could, and she went to sleep. The next morning, the test seemed easy. Later that week, Carmen found out she had gotten an A on the test—her first A all year.

Another example of good stress is the way you feel the night before a big test. You might find it kind of hard to sleep. You might not be very hungry. As long as those feelings don't keep you awake all night or keep you from eating at all, then this is healthy stress. Your symptoms will probably help you study harder and even do better on the test.

Sometimes one event can cause different people to experience different kinds of stress. Imagine a roller coaster ride packed with kids. **Some of the kids are probably waving their hands in the air, hooting and hollering, and having the time of their lives. But others are tightly gripping the roller coaster car, eyes squeezed shut, waiting for the ride to be over.** *All the kids are experiencing symptoms of stress.* Their hearts are beating faster. They are focused only on the moment and the thrill—or nightmare—of the ride.

Stress Can Be Bad: José's Story

All year, José had done really well in math class. But now, his class was studying geometry— and it didn't make any sense to José. He was too embarrassed to ask anyone for help. So he just stopped studying. Instead of doing homework, he

began to spend his evenings playing his favorite video game. He loved playing his game. But he started feeling really bad about math class. One day, his teacher asked him why he hadn't done his math homework. José just turned red and tried to think of an excuse. After that, he didn't want to go to math class at all. For three days in a row, he pretended he was sick. His mom let him stay home. He wasn't really sick. But he did start to feel terrible. He got a huge stomachache every time he thought about math class—which seemed like every minute of the day. He didn't know what to do.

When Stress Gets Major

Major stress is the kind of stress that seems to go on and on. If you feel like you have too much homework every single day, then you will feel stressed every single day. If you feel like your life is out of control, you will also feel stresses. For instance, maybe you find yourself running around like a crazy person every morning, hunting down your backpack, shoes, hat, and whatever else you need for school. Or maybe you feel like your days are so filled with school, sports, and chores that you never get time to just chill out. These kinds of feeling will also cause stress. But it's not usually the sweaty-palms, beating-heart kind of stress.

This kind of stress might keep you awake almost every night. **It might give you headaches. It might make you feel cranky.** You might get stomachaches or feel sick all over.

There are lots of reasons that kids feel major stress. Take a look at the list of things that stress kids out on the next page. How many of these events or feelings have you experienced? Did they make you feel stressed? A lot of times, bad stress doesn't just come from one event. It comes from many different things. If you feel like you are having trouble at home, at school, and with your best friend, you are going to feel stressed.

People deal with major stress in lots of different ways. Some people lose their appetites and hardly eat anything. Other people turn to food— *especially junk food.*

DID YOU KNOW?
Stress is one of the causes of obesity—the condition of being very overweight.

Things That Stress Kids Out

tests

having trouble with schoolwork

trying new activities

an illness or death in the family

having family members who fight with one another

a divorce in the family

performing in front of others

the death of a pet

moving to a new neighborhood

feeling like their parents are always picking on them

feeling like they don't have any friends

peer pressure

being bullied or teased

feeling like their best friend doesn't want to be friends anymore

Some people stop feeling tired and have trouble getting to sleep at night. Other people feel tired all the time and never want to get out of bed.

When stress gets really bad, people sometimes start avoiding things. If you're always fighting with your parents, you might start locking yourself in your bedroom.

This might seem to make it easier to get through the day. But it probably won't help you get along with your parents. If you aren't doing well at school, you might stop trying altogether. You might even think about skipping school. This might seem easier than facing school when you haven't done your homework. But of course, it will really only make you get further behind.

This is the kind of stress that can harm you over time. But it's also the kind of stress you can do something about. Once you know what stress is, you can recognize when you feel stressed. And once you understand what makes you feel stressed, you can make changes in your life to limit that stress. Chapter 3 gives you some tips to help.

There are other kinds of stress that you don't have much control over. If a big change happens in your life, you are going to be stressed. If someone you know dies or you move to a new town, you will have stress. You can't do much about the situation. But you can help yourself get through it. Chapter 4 gives you some tips for coping with really major stress.

Chapter 2

WHAT'S Really GOING ON?

So what really happens when you feel *Stress?*

Is your mind just playing tricks on you?

Is stress a sign that you can't deal with your own life?

No! In fact, stress is your body's way of dealing head-on with life's pressures. It's a method of problem solving that humans have used for more than one million years. People first began experiencing stress when they lived in caves. They weren't worried about tests or making the basketball team then. But they did have plenty to worry about. Floods, tornadoes, and other weather events often appeared out of nowhere. Ferocious animals who enjoyed a tasty meal of people were everywhere. In order to survive, cave-dwelling people had to react quickly to these threats.

DID YOU KNOW?
The term stress *is short for* distress, *a word that comes from the Latin word meaning "to draw or pull apart."*

Luckily, even the earliest human bodies were equipped with a type of stress reaction. It's called the *fight-or-flight response*. When cave dwellers were surprised or worried, they had two options. They could fight. Or they could run. And they often didn't have much time to decide on the best option. If a big hungry beast was lurking outside the cave, people had to act quickly. Fighting prehistoric beasts was no easy feat. But neither was running from one. To do either, people needed all their strength.

The fight-or-flight response helps give people strength. It energizes them and prepares them to *escape* or to *fight*. As soon as the brain senses danger, it goes into fight-or-flight mode. It makes special chemicals to give the body more energy. It tells the heart to beat faster. This sends extra blood to the muscles, preparing them for work. Thanks to the fight-or-flight response, cave dwellers had a chance to either face danger or flee from it. This automatic response probably saved us from dying out over the years. Let's take a closer look at what's really going on.

Inside the Brain

Stress—just like everything you think, say, or do—starts in the brain. The brain is the body's pilot. It figures out what's going on around the body and inside the body. Then it tells all the other body parts what to do.

When the brain senses any change—either inside or outside the body—it springs into action. Sometimes the change is a familiar change. Then the brain knows just what to tell the body. For instance, if the brain smells pancakes cooking, it might check in with the stomach. Then it might send some signals that the body is hungry. Before you know it, your stomach might be growling.

Quick Reaction

Often your body will start reacting to stress before your mind even recognizes the stressful event. Think about what happens when you hear a strange noise in the middle of the night. Doesn't your heart start beating fast before you even have time to imagine what could have caused the noise? That's your body, getting ready to fight or flee!

But other times, the brain might not be quite sure how to react to a change. This could be an unexpected change, like getting hit in the head with a soccer ball. Or it could be a confusing change, like hearing something unusual in the middle of the night. On the other hand, it could be an anticipated change that your brain just hasn't figured out yet—like a math test. In all of these cases, the brain is likely to go into fight-or-flight mode.

Once the brain decides to get into fight-or-flight mode, things start happening automatically. Of course, when you're talking about the brain, automatic does not mean simple. Take a look at the steps involved when the brain sends out the fight-or-flight message.

Seeing Clearly

Even the eyes are affected by the fight-or-flight response. While the rest of the body prepares to fight or flee, the eyes do their part by focusing all their energy into being able to see as clearly as possible. You may notice that your pupils dilate—or grow larger—in times of stress.

When the fight-or-flight response gets triggered, chemical reactions cause a pair of organs called the adrenal glands to produce the hormone cortisol. At the same time, the brain sends out a chemical called acetylcholine. This chemical tells the adrenal glands to release two more hormones: adrenaline and noradrenaline. **Adrenaline**, **noradrenaline**, and **cortisol** give the body the extra energy it needs to deal with a stressful event. **Let's take a closer look at these three hormones.**

Adrenaline

Adrenaline speeds up the heart. When the heart speeds up, it pumps extra blood to deliver extra oxygen to the muscles. This gives the muscles an extra boost of energy.

Noradrenaline

This hormone helps adrenaline do its job. It increases blood pressure. It speeds up breathing. It also slows down blood flow to the parts of the body that are not important for the fight-or-flight response. This means the stomach doesn't get any extra blood—but the muscles in the legs and arms do.

Cortisol

Cortisol helps you keep up your extra energy. It keeps you energized for a long enough time to let you deal with the stressful situation.

With the help of these three hormones, your body can prepare itself to deal with just about any stressful event. Many different parts of your body join in these preparations.

It's Not All in Your Head

Stress starts in the brain, but it quickly travels through
your whole body. Signs of stress—like a fast heartbeat or a
stomachache—are not imaginary. They are real. They result from
the fight-or-flight response that started in your brain.

You know those hormones that your brain releases to give your
body extra strength to deal with stress? Well, they aren't the
only part of your body that works hard when you get stressed.
When your breath quickens and your heart pounds, your body
temperature goes up. This causes your body's automatic cooling
system to come on. You may start to sweat or notice that your
hands feel clammy. That's your
body's air conditioner at work.

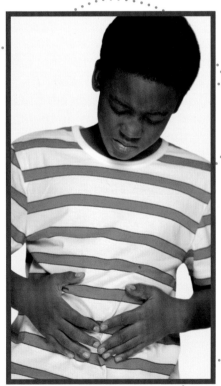

Meanwhile, other parts of your
body temporarily shut down. This
helps save energy to use where
it's needed most. Your digestive
system takes a rest during
times of stress. This means your
stomach stops digesting food.
If you haven't eaten in a while,
you'll notice that you don't feel
hungry when you are stressed. **If
you've just eaten, you might
feel like your stomach is
churning. That's because the
stomach acids—which had
been hard at work breaking
down your last meal—are now
just sloshing around in your
stomach.**

Cooling Down After Stress

It's great that your body has an emergency plan for dealing with stress. But a body can't function for *too* long in emergency mode. Getting back to normal is an important part of the stress response. In fact, the act of getting back to normal even has its own name: *the relaxation response.*

The relaxation response is the body's way of stopping the fight-or-flight response. It begins in the brain—just like the fight-or-flight response. Once the stress has passed, the brain releases more chemicals. These chemicals overtake the adrenaline, noradrenaline, and cortisol produced earlier. This helps to reverse all the stress symptoms. The heart slows down. Breathing slows too. Soon the body is back to normal.

When your body's *relaxation response* kicks in shortly after the fight-or-flight response, your body stays pretty balanced. It gains the short-term benefits of fight-or-flight—extra focus and energy to get through a new situation. But it doesn't get stuck in this highly stressful mode.

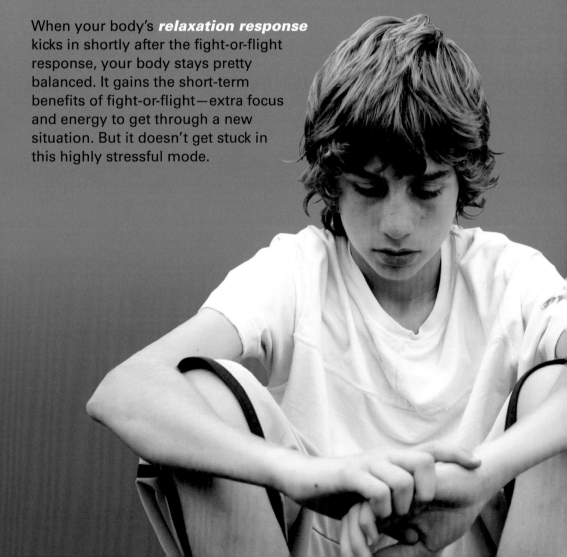

Stress Overload

What happens when your relaxation response doesn't kick in after a stressful event? Or what if you experience many fight-or-flight events, all one after the other?

It's one thing to get stressed about a test at the end of a week. But if every day is filled with stress, it can lead to problems. You can probably imagine why being stressed all the time wouldn't be good for you. *Let's take a closer look at exactly how long-term stress affects the body.*

The main result of too much stress comes from the stress hormones. Usually, these hormones get stopped in their tracks during the relaxation response. But if they don't, you can end up with a stress-hormone overdose. This would make you feel jumpy all the time. But other things would be going on too. Having too much adrenaline for a long time can lead to heart disease. And too much cortisol in your body can slow down another hormone called serotonin. Serotonin is important because it controls your body clock. Your body clock is an internal system that prepares your body for sleep at night. It also directs your body to wake up in the morning. Without enough serotonin, your body clock can't function well. It can't tell your body when to sleep and when to wake up. This can affect your body's ability to stay healthy and fight off illness. It can affect your brain's ability to think clearly too.

Chapter 3

KEEPING
Stress
IN CHECK

There's no doubt about it.

Stress can REALLY mess with you.

Unfortunately, stressful events happen all around you. You probably can't get through many days without stress. But did you know that you have the power to limit the way your body reacts to stress?

It's true. If you take care of your health, you can keep all the small stresses of life from turning into major stresses. Keeping your body in top shape will give you extra energy for dealing with the events that can trigger stress responses. **Eating right, exercising,** and **getting enough sleep** are the three biggies when it comes to staying healthy. Keeping away from unhealthful substances such as drugs and alcohol is also key to remaining stress free.

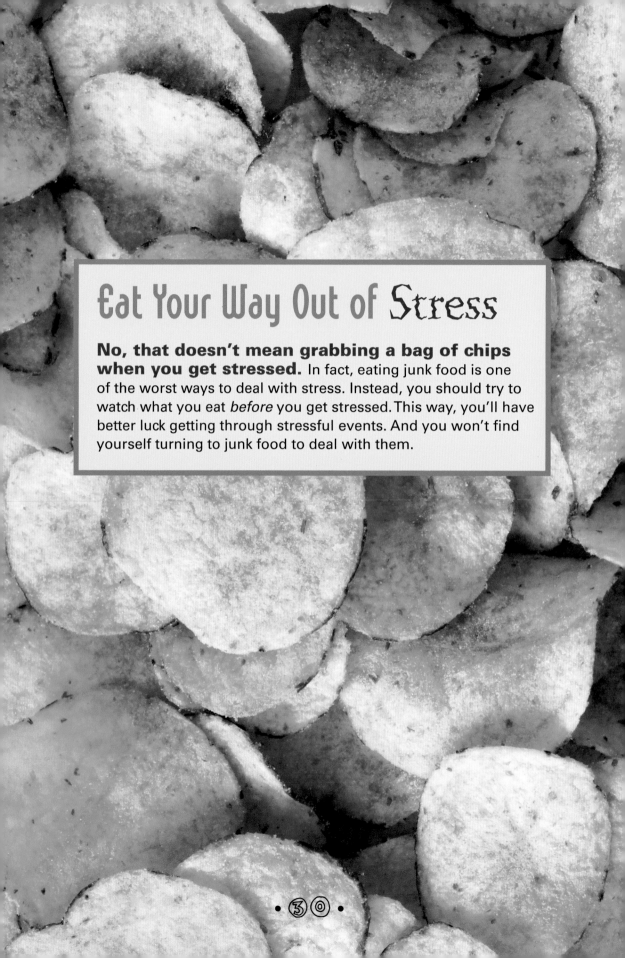

Eat Your Way Out of Stress

No, that doesn't mean grabbing a bag of chips when you get stressed. In fact, eating junk food is one of the worst ways to deal with stress. Instead, you should try to watch what you eat *before* you get stressed. This way, you'll have better luck getting through stressful events. And you won't find yourself turning to junk food to deal with them.

Beware of Sweets

When you feel yourself start to get stressed, a candy bar or a couple of cookies might seem like a quick way to feel better. But be careful. A sweet treat can lead to a quick crash. Your body processes sugar quickly. This leads to a "sugar buzz," where you may feel full of energy for a short time. But what goes up must come down. That energy spike from a sugar buzz will be followed by a "sugar crash." And that will make you feel tired, cranky, and not at all prepared to deal with stress.

One of the best things about eating healthfully is that it's pretty easy to do it well. The United States Department of Agriculture (USDA) has come up with a simple guide to help you watch what you eat. The guide is called **MyPyramid**. It's a big triangle that shows the five major food groups. The groups are:

grains (this includes foods like whole-wheat breads and pastas)

vegetables (think bell peppers, sweet potatoes, and spinach)

fruits (such as apples, oranges, and bananas)

milk (including yogurt, cheese, and—you guessed it!—milk)

meat and beans (chicken, eggs, nuts, and beans are just a few of the foods that fit into this group)

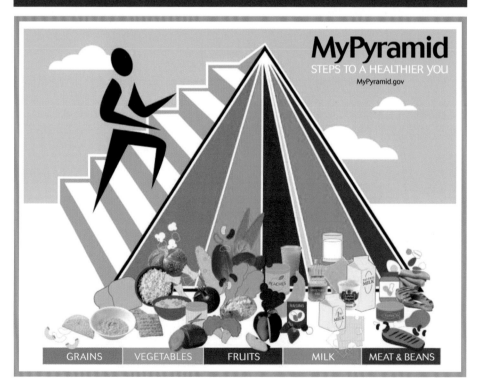

Oils

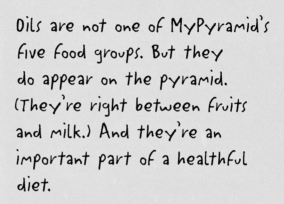

Oils are not one of MyPyramid's five food groups. But they do appear on the pyramid. (They're right between fruits and milk.) And they're an important part of a healthful diet.

How can you get the oils you need? Try eating fish or nuts. These foods contain oils. Or snack on a freshly baked whole-grain roll dipped in olive oil. Olive oil is a healthful—and tasty— alternative to butter.

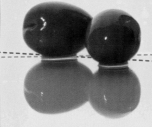

Making sure you eat foods from all five groups every day will go a long way toward keeping you healthy. Choosing foods from the five food groups may not come naturally to you at first. But once you get started watching what you eat, it will begin to seem like second nature. Maybe you already do a good job of choosing foods from three or four of the groups. Then you can start thinking about how you can round out your diet by adding in the other one or two.

If your eating habits are a *long* way off from MyPyramid's recommendations, don't stress about it! To get started on a more healthful eating plan, talk to an adult who has good eating habits. Or try talking to a doctor. Ask for some advice on how to begin taking care of your body from the inside out. When you start having more energy and less stress, you'll be glad you did.

How Much Food from Each Group Do You Need?

Everyone's nutritional needs are different. But the boxes below show about how much food from each group a nine- to twelve-year-old might need. You may need more or less depending on factors like your activity level and whether you're a boy or girl. To create a MyPyramid plan especially for you, visit http://www.mypyramid.gov.

Meat and Beans: 5 ounces (141 grams)

Milk: 3 cups

Fruits: 1½ cups

Grains: 6 ounces (170 g)

Vegetables: 2½ cups

Pump Up Your Energy

When it comes to being healthy, getting enough exercise is just as important as eating right. Here's a cool fact about exercise: it uses up energy, but it also creates more energy. **If you get regular exercise, your body will feel more powerful and more energized.**

When you don't get enough exercise, your body doesn't feel energized. Instead, you feel sluggish all the time.

Besides giving you energy, exercise has another benefit: it makes your whole body feel better. It keeps your blood pumping through your body. It helps your lungs breathe more deeply. It can even improve your mood. That's right! Exercise can make you feel happier. That's because exercising releases chemicals called endorphins. Endorphins are often called the feel-good hormone. They create a happy feeling whenever they are traveling through your blood stream.

The best thing about exercise is that it's actually a fun way to do something good for yourself. There are as many different ways to exercise as there are people. Are you a social person who likes to spend time with friends? Just getting together with friends and going for a walk can be good exercise. If the weather won't let you walk outside, put on some music and dance for a half hour. You'll have a blast and get good exercise at the same time. Are you a person who likes a challenge? Join a team sport like soccer or basketball. Do you like to spend time alone with your thoughts—or your music? Take a run or a bike ride. **Whatever you decide to do, make it a part of your daily routine.** Kids and teenagers need sixty minutes of moderate exercise every day to stay healthy.

Give It a Rest

Sleeping may seem less complicated than exercising or eating right. *But it's just as important to good health.* Sleep gives your body a chance to recover from a day's activities. It gives you energy to get through the next day. That means having energy to deal with new things, big changes, or tricky situations—all the things that can cause stress. Getting enough sleep makes you feel calmer too. That's because it helps to balance your body's energy level.

DID YOU KNOW?
Sleep not only gives your body energy. It also gives your brain more power. Scientists recently discovered that getting a full night's sleep before a test can help you get a higher score than staying up late to study.

Sleep also gives your brain a chance to think things over. Sometimes a problem that seems *huge* before you go to bed might feel not so huge in the morning. This might be because you feel better and have more energy to face the problem in the morning. But it may also be because your brain was at work thinking of solutions—even though you were fast asleep.

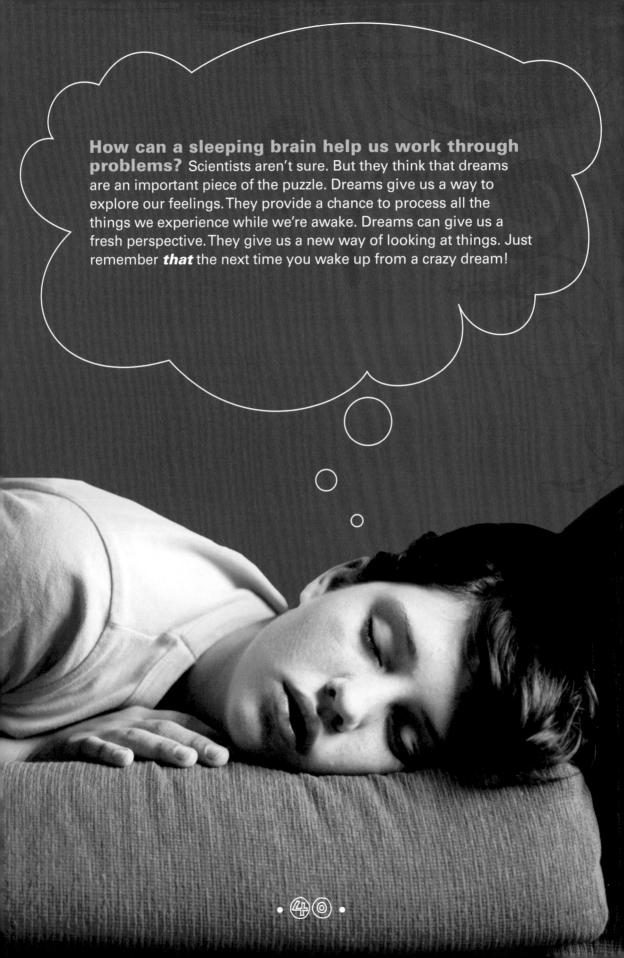

How can a sleeping brain help us work through problems? Scientists aren't sure. But they think that dreams are an important piece of the puzzle. Dreams give us a way to explore our feelings. They provide a chance to process all the things we experience while we're awake. Dreams can give us a fresh perspective. They give us a new way of looking at things. Just remember *that* the next time you wake up from a crazy dream!

How Much Sleep Do You Need?

Most kids need about **ten hours** of sleep a night. Some need a little more. Others need a little less. Do you get enough sleep? Or do you often feel tired and unable to concentrate during the day? If you're eating right and exercising, you should be able to keep up your energy throughout the day. So if you're doing those two things and still feel tired, you probably need to ramp up your sleeping hours.

Here are some tips to help you get enough sleep to keep your stress level low.

❶ Set a regular bedtime.
Getting to bed at about the same time every night helps your body get the most out of sleep. It can be tempting to stay up later than normal on Friday and Saturday nights. But if you stay up *too* late, it may be tough to get up for school on Monday morning! Your weekend bedtime should be no more than one hour later than your weeknight bedtime.

❷ Follow the same routine each night.
Include the things you have to do (brushing teeth, washing face) as well as something that helps you relax. (Try reading or listening to music for fifteen minutes just before lights out.) This will help prepare your body for sleep.

❸ Create a good sleep environment.
Don't sleep in your clothes. Or on the couch. Or with the lights on. Don't leave music or the television on either. Your body needs calm, dark, and quiet to get good sleep.

Just Say No

Most kids know that **drugs**, **cigarettes**, and **alcohol** are bad for them. But some still turn to drugs when life is difficult. Drugs might seem like they help with problems. But really all they do is make your brain unable to think through problems clearly. And of course, they can damage your brain, heart, and nervous system. All of this leads to bigger problems—and more stress—in the long run.

Staying healthy by staying away from drugs is pretty simple. But using drugs isn't the only behavior that can increase stress. Arguing and feeling mad at other people can raise your tension level too. Saying no to those feelings is a good way to keep stress away. **Once you start feeling stressed, it can be hard to stop negative feelings. But you have the power to limit how much those feelings control you—and your stress levels.** Check out chapter 4 for some tips on staying cool when you feel hot and bothered.

Go CAFFEINE free

Did you know it's not just illegal drugs that can harm you? Take caffeine, for example. Caffeine is a drug found in drinks such as colas. It gives you a burst of energy. It might seem like that would be helpful for dealing with stress. But the way caffeine works in your body makes you more likely to get stressed. Caffeine speeds up your heart and nervous system. This can cause anxiety. It can make it harder for you to relax. Check the labels of your favorite drinks. If they contain caffeine, try switching to water or something else that's caffeine free. Your body will thank you!

Chapter 4

WHAT TO DO WHEN Major Stress HITS

If you're like most kids,

you are going to get hit with some major stress *at some point in your life.*

You can take care of your body by **eating right**, **sleeping**, and **exercising**. This will help you keep your stress level low. But every once in a while, some big whammy might come along and knock you off your feet. Usually the biggest whammies are things you can't control. You can't help it when someone close to you gets sick or even dies. You can't help it when your parents fight or get divorced.

But you **can help** how you deal with these problems. You have lots of power over your own actions. You also have the power to focus on positive parts of your life. You can do this even when everything seems overwhelming.

Change What You Can

Sometimes it may feel like you have no control over events in your life. But really, you almost always have some control. Realizing what you can control—and then controlling it—can really help keep stress down.

Picture this. It's a new school year, and you're in a new class. Only none of your friends from last year are in your class. Instead, it seems like all the kids this year are kind of scary. They're bigger than you. And they all seem to know one another. So you don't talk much at all during school. But then some of the other kids start to tease you. They call you names and laugh at you because you're quiet in class.

This is the kind of thing that can cause major stress. It can also seem like you have no control. But think about it. You do have options. For one thing, you could punch the next person who teases you. But what will that solve? You'll get in trouble and probably get suspended from school. Sounds stressful!

What's another option? You could try to ignore your feelings. You could just keep on being quiet in class and not tell anyone about the teasing. ***But what would happen then?*** The bullies in your class might keep teasing you. You'd probably get more stressed about going to school. Since you didn't tell anyone how you're feeling, you might think nobody understands. Feeling alone often brings on the worst parts of stress. You might start to get headaches and stomachaches. Soon you might have trouble sleeping.

But what if you tried another option? There actually are a few other options:

What if you talked to someone about how alone you felt in your new class? You could talk to a friend, someone in your family, a school counselor, or a teacher. They could help you figure out a plan to make things better.

Or what if you made a decision to find one thing you really like about school? Maybe you really like music, or you really like science. Focusing on things you like can make the things you don't like feel less important.

Or what if you made small changes about how you act in class? Maybe it would work to talk to the kids who are being mean to you. Maybe it will turn out that they feel alone too and don't know what to say. Or maybe you could talk to another person in the class. Maybe you'd soon find a group of friends.

Not all of these ideas would work for every person. But at least one of them would probably work in any situation. **The important thing to remember is that you have the power to make change.** Sometimes stress can make you feel like you don't have any options. But you almost always do. When you take positive action, you increase the chances of changing things to the way you'd like them to be. In the rest of this chapter, you can read more about different ideas to try in different stressful situations. One or more of them will probably work for you the next time you are faced with major stress.

Positive focus

If something in your life is stressing you out, take a moment to think about something else that's going well. Sometimes just reminding yourself about good things in your life can lower your stress level.

Talk It Over

There's no doubt about it—sharing stress can be the best way to beat it. This is especially true for major stress. Major stress—unlike a spelling test, for instance—is probably not going to go away on its own. But talking things over with someone can help you figure out how to deal with it. Sometimes other people can help you see events more clearly. In some cases, it helps to talk to someone else who knows and understands whatever is stressing you out. Other times, it's best to get an opinion from someone who is not involved in the situation.

Next time you feel yourself begin to get stressed, think about who you can talk to. Sometimes talking to a friend can be best. Other times, talking to someone in your family works better. This could be a sibling, a parent, or even a grandparent or aunt and uncle who live far away. Chances are, they would be happy to help you deal with any stress in your life. If you don't have trusted family members, or you'd rather not talk to them, think about other adults in your life. You can ask a teacher, a coach, a neighbor, or a religious leader if they would mind talking something over with you. Sometimes—especially those times when it seems like there's nobody to talk to—talking to a counselor or therapist can help. Counselors and therapists are experts in how to deal with stress. They can help you work through your problem and find ways to keep yourself healthy while you're under big stress. Lots of kids go to counselors or therapists if their parents get divorced, if someone close to them dies, or during other stressful events.

If It feels Like a Big Deal, It *Is* a Big Deal

Sometimes you may find yourself feeling stressed about something that you think you shouldn't be stressed about. For instance, everybody expects you to be stressed if someone in your family dies. But what if your pet snake dies? Some people might think that shouldn't bother you. They might even tell you to get over it. But the death of a pet can be very  stressful. It's a big change and a big loss in your life. And stress is your body's way of dealing with change. So, of course you might feel overwhelmed if your pet snake dies. Remember to listen to your own body's clues about how you feel. If you feel stressed, try some of the ideas in this chapter to treat your stress. Don't listen when other people tell you how you should feel.

Practice Relaxing

Remember the relaxation response? It's supposed to follow right after your body's fight-or-flight reaction. It helps your body return to normal. But sometimes, especially when you're going through major stress, your relaxation response doesn't get started. Then your stress response just keeps on going. This can really wear you out! Luckily, you can jump-start your relaxation response yourself.

Sometimes relaxing is as simple as doing something you enjoy. If you play an instrument or a sport, you might find that those activities calm you down. **Zoning out for a few minutes in front of the television or a video game is OK too. Just make sure you don't spend *too* long in front of media. After more than 20 or 30 minutes, it stops being relaxing and can actually start to raise your stress levels.**

DID YOU KNOW?
Laughter really can be good medicine. Experts think that keeping a sense of humor— and letting yourself laugh out loud when life seems really crazy—can help reduce stress.

You can also check out a relaxing art form like yoga or meditation. Yoga is an ancient religious practice from India. In yoga you hold your body in different poses to make your body more relaxed, stronger, and more flexible. Meditating is when you clear your mind by concentrating on one thing, such as counting or chanting a word over and over. Try yoga and meditation together or separately to see which relaxes you the most.

Acupressure

People have been feeling stress since the time of cave dwellers. And they've been coming up with ways to treat it for almost as long. Thousands of years ago in Asia, people used acupressure to relieve stress.

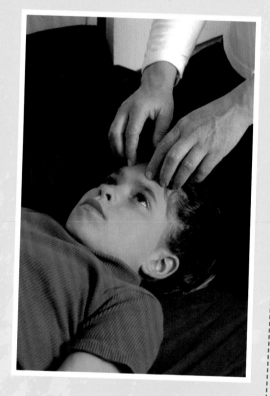

Acupressure is the art of applying pressure to specific spots on the body to make people feel better. These spots are called pressure points. The spot right above your nose and between your eyebrows is a pressure point. Try pressing on that spot the next time you feel yourself getting stressed. See if you begin to feel more relaxed.

Get Organized

Sometimes it's not one particular thing that causes stress. A bunch of little things can add up to big stress. Is too much homework, too many activities, or just too much going on stressing you out? You can take action. Start by making a list of everything you have to do in a day or in a week. Then make a schedule. Give yourself time to complete everything on your list. Don't forget to add in time to exercise, relax, and hang out with friends. Can't fit in everything on your list? Then it's time to prioritize—rank things by how important they are. Can you reschedule some things for the next day or the next week?

Another way to manage stress is to organize your things. Think about it. Are you late for school nearly every day because you can't find your shoes, your backpack, or your homework? That's a high-stress way to start the day. By keeping your things organized, you can cut out all that time spent running around in circles. Then you can spend your extra minutes finishing your breakfast or even listening to a favorite song before you head out. **Sounds like a better way to start the day, doesn't it?**

Everyone has stressful events in their life.

Some people feel more stress than others. But everyone feels some stress.

If you're a person who naturally has a low level of stress, then you're pretty lucky. But if you're a person who naturally feels a lot of stress, it doesn't mean you're unlucky. It just means you might have to work a little harder to manage your stress. Knowing how your body reacts to stress can help you know when your stress is getting high. And knowing some ways to deal with stress will help you. The next time you are feeling stressed out and overwhelmed, remember that it's just your body reacting naturally to change. And focus on the things you can do to keep your stress in check.

You'll find that stress is a little easier to manage when you know what you're dealing with.

Now that you've read all about stress, try this fun quiz to see how much you know. Please record your answers on a separate sheet of paper. (Answers appear at the bottom of page 58.)

1. **Which of the following statements about stress is true?**

   a. Stress is always good for you. In fact, it's the best thing that can happen to a kid.

   b. Stress is the Worst Thing Ever! There is absolutely nothing good about stress.

   c. Stress can be good in small doses and harmful when it gets out of control.

2. **The fight-or-flight response is another name for:**

   a. The human stress response

   b. What birds do when it rains

   c. What you should think about when someone tries to start a fight with you

3. **Major stress might cause you to:**

   a. Lose your appetite and have trouble sleeping

   b. Overeat and feel tired all the time

   c. Both a and b

4. **Which three hormones give the body extra energy to help it deal with stress?**

   a. Noradrenaline, hyperadrenaline, and serotonin

   b. Adrenaline, noradrenaline, and cortisol

   c. Adrenaline, serotonin, and endorphins

5. **The following body system temporarily shuts down in times of stress:**

   a. The nervous system

   b. The digestive system

   c. The circulatory system

6. **How much sleep do most kids need to stay healthy and keep their stress level low?**

   a. About ten hours a night

   b. About eight hours a night

   c. Kids don't need any sleep

7. What kinds of foods might help you feel less stressed?

a. Fruits and vegetables

b. Sugary desserts

c. Drinks with extra caffeine

8. What's the best thing to do when you're feeling stressed out?

a. Play a video game

b. Try to ignore your feelings

c. Try to relax by reading, playing a sport, or doing some yoga

9. If you feel like you have too much going on in your life, it might help to:

a. Make a list of everything you have to do

b. Try to organize your things

c. Both a and b

10. Talking with someone about your stress:

a. Can only make things worse

b. Can be the best way to beat it

c. Is a good idea only if you've already tried everything else.

Yoga

Yoga can be a great way to relax your mind and your body—and say good-bye to stress overload. One yoga pose is called the snake. You can give the snake a try the next time you're feeling stressed. Here's how:

1. Lie on your back with your knees bent. Keep your legs together and the bottoms of your feet on the floor.

2. Press your lower back to the floor. Keep your upper back relaxed and your arms at your sides.

3. Breathe in deeply. Holding your breath in, tighten your stomach, and count to three.

4. Let your breath out and relax

5. Repeat ten times.

Feel relaxed?

Glossary

adrenaline: a hormone produced by the adrenal glands. Adrenaline speeds up the heart.

body clock: an internal system that prepares the body for sleep and waking

caffeine: a drug that speeds up your heart and nervous system

cortisol: a hormone produced by the adrenal glands. Cortisol helps you keep your energy up in times of stress.

counselor: a professional who is trained to help with problems and give advice

endorphin: a hormone that creates a feeling of well being. Your body releases endorphins when you exercise.

fight-or-flight response: a stress response that prepares people to either escape from a distressing situation or fight against it

meditation: the practice of clearing your mind by concentrating on one thing, such as counting or chanting the same word over and over

MyPyramid: The United States Department of Agriculture's guide to healthful eating. MyPyramid breaks foods into five major groups: grains, vegetables, fruits, milk, and meat and beans.

noradrenaline: a hormone produced by the adrenal glands. Noradrenaline helps adrenaline to do its job.

relaxation response: the body's way of stopping the fight-or-flight response. When the relaxation response kicks in, your heart and breathing rates slow down.

serotonin: a hormone that controls the body clock

yoga: an ancient religious practice from India in which you hold your body in different poses. Yoga can make your body stronger, more relaxed, and more flexible.

Selected Bibliography

Brynie, Faith. *The Physical Brain*. Woodbridge, CT: Blackbirch Press, 2001.

Culbert, Timothy, and Rebecca Kajander. *Be the Boss of Your Stress*. Minneapolis: Free Spirit Publishing, 2007.

Fox, Annie, and Ruth Kirschner. *Too Stressed to Think?* Minneapolis: Free Spirit Publishing, 2005.

Hipp, Earl. *Fighting Invisible Tigers: A Stress Management Guide for Teens*. Minneapolis: Free Spirit Publishing, 1995.

Hyman, Bruce M., and Cherry Pedrick. *Anxiety Disorders*. Minneapolis: Twenty-First Century Books, 2006.

Nemours Foundation. "The Story on Stress." *KidsHealth*. 2008. http://www.kidshealth.org/kid/feeling/emotion/stress.html (February 22, 2008).

Roosevelt University. "Facts about Stress and Stress Management." *Roosevelt University*. 2006. http://www.roosevelt.edu/stress/facts.htm (February 22, 2008).

Sapolsky, Robert M. *Why Zebras Don't Get Ulcers: An Updated Guide to Stress, Stress-Related Diseases, and Coping*. New York: W. H. Freeman and Co., 1998.

Witkin, Georgia. *KidStress: What It Is, How It Feels, How to Help*. New York: Viking Penguin, 1999.

Learn More about Stress

Ayer, Eleanor H. *Everything You Need to Know about Stress*. New York: Rosen, 2001. Ayer provides tips on dealing with family problems, school issues, and other common sources of stress.

Crist, James J. *What to Do When You're Scared & Worried: A Guide for Kids*. Minneapolis: Free Spirit Publishing, 2004. This title examines where fears and worries come from and how to deal with them.

Culbert, Timothy, and Rebecca Kajander. *Be the Boss of Your Stress: Self-Care for Kids*. Minneapolis: Free Spirit Publishing, 2007. Read about some steps that young people can take to control their stress and improve the quality of their lives.

Hyde, Margaret O., and Elizabeth H. Forsyth. *Stress 101: An Overview for Teens*. Minneapolis: Twenty-First Century Books, 2008. This in-depth title is packed with information on stress for kids and teens.

It's My Life
http://pbskids.org/itsmylife/index.html
This website offers useful information on friends, family, health, emotions, and other topics.

KidsHealth
http://kidshealth.org/kid
Visit KidsHealth to find articles on a variety of issues, including stress, text anxiety, and getting along with family members.

Moser, Adolph. *Don't Pop Your Cork on Mondays!: The Children's Anti-Stress Book*. Kansas City, MO: Landmark Editions, 1988. This classic book for helping kids deal with stress has lots of timeless information on the causes and effects of stress.

Romain, Trevor, and Elizabeth Verdick. *Stress Can Really Get on Your Nerves!* Minneapolis: Free Spirit Publishing, 2000. Read more about stress and how you can manage it.

Photo/Illustration Acknowledgments

The images in this book are used with the permission of: © Omni Photo Communications Inc./Index Stock Imagery/Photolibrary, p. 4; © Jaimie Travis/DK Stock/Getty Images, p. 6; © iStockphoto.com/Jim Kolaczko, p. 8; © Bubbles Photography/Alamy, pp. 9, 54; © Chris Clinton/Taxi/Getty Images, pp. 10, 52 (top left); © Anton Vengo/SuperStock, pp. 11, 44; © ATABOY/The Image Bank/Getty Images, p. 12; © Julie Fisher/Taxi/Getty Images, p. 13; © Michael Goldman/The Image Bank/Getty Images, p. 14; © Dennis MacDonald/Alamy, p. 15; © Erin Patrice O'Brien/Taxi/Getty Images, p. 16 (top left and bottom); © Catherine Ledner/Riser/Getty Images, p. 16 (top right); © Shioguchi/Taxi Japan/Getty Images, p. 17 (top); © Lisette Le Bon/SuperStock, p. 17 (bottom); © iStockphoto.com/Izabela Habur, p. 18; ©Todd Strand/Independent Picture Service, p. 22; ©Tom Le Goff/Digital Vision/Getty Images, p. 24; © iStockphoto.com/Jane Norton, p. 25; © Ian Shaw/Alamy, p. 26; © Ty Allison/Taxi/Getty Images, p. 28; © iStockphoto.com/Mark Atkins, p. 29; © iStockphoto.com/Daemys, p. 30; © Photodisc/Getty Images, pp. 31, 34, 35 (top left and right), 39; Agricultural Research Service, USDA, p. 32; © Ekaterina Fribus/Dreamstime.com, p. 33; © Comstock Images, p. 35 (top center and bottom right); © image100 Ltd./CORBIS, p. 35 (bottom left); © Nicolas Russell/Photographer's Choice/Getty Images, p. 37 (top); ©Tom Stewart/CORBIS, p. 37 (bottom); © George Doyle/Stockbyte/Getty Images, p. 38; © age fotostock/SuperStock, pp. 40, 42 (right), 57; © iStockphoto.com, p. 42 (left); © iStockphoto.com/Bonnie Schupp, p. 45; © Nicholas Prior/Taxi/Getty Images, p. 46; © Kate Powers/Taxi/Getty Images, p. 47; © Photofusion Picture Library/Alamy, p. 50; © Leland Bobbe/Photonica/Getty Images, p. 51; © Reggie Casagrande/Taxi/Getty Images, p. 52 (right); © Chris Stock Photography/Alamy, p. 52 (bottom left); © Ruth Jenkinson/Dorling Kindersley/Getty Images, p. 55; © John Birsdall/The Image Works, p. 58 (top); © Stephen Wilkes/The Image Bank/Getty Images, p. 58 (bottom); © Julie Caruso, p. 59.

Cover: © Royalty-Free/CORBIS.

About the Author

Sandy Donovan has written many books for young readers, including *Stay Clear!: What You Should Know about Skin Care*. She lives in Minneapolis, Minnesota, with her family, Henry, Gus, and Eric.